Original title:
Rooted and Radiant

Copyright © 2025 Creative Arts Management OÜ
All rights reserved.

Author: Riley Donovan
ISBN HARDBACK: 978-1-80581-771-0
ISBN PAPERBACK: 978-1-80581-298-2
ISBN EBOOK: 978-1-80581-771-0

Blooming Beyond Burrows

In the depths of dirt, a sprout finds cheer,
Wiggling its leaves, it shouts, "I'm here!"
With worms as friends, they dance in glee,
Singing to the sun, wild and free.

A dandelion dreams of being a prize,
While a timid tulip just mumbles and sighs.
They laugh at the clouds, a curious crew,
"We're blooming buddies, just look at our view!"

Subterranean Splendor

Down in the soil, where the roots gossip,
The carrots' tales make everyone flip.
"I'm orange and crunchy, the king of all snacks!"
"Oh please," says the beet, "You're just a bit lax!"

Moles steal the scene with their sleek little togs,
While mushrooms gossip with the sassiest frogs.
In this underground party, the laughs never end,
They toast with their cups, celebrating each friend!

The Glow of Resilience

A daisy stands tall, despite all the rain,
"Just splash on my petals; I'll dance through the pain!"
While daisies sway, the grass starts to trip,
"Hey! Watch yourself, don't give me a slip!"

In the face of a storm, they spin and they twirl,
"We thrive on the chaos, give it a whirl!"
The sun peeks through clouds and the flowers unite,
With giggles and grins, they bask in the light!

Embracing Sun and Soil

In a garden of laughter, the sun meets the dirt,
With flowers all gabbing, their petals all flirt.
A sunflower grins, as tall as can be,
While a shy little sprout hides behind a tree.

The flowers debate, "Who's the best bloom?"
"Let's grow big and bright, and light up the room!"
They twirl in the breeze, sharing jokes in the sun,
With roots tangled tight, they all laugh as one!

Interwoven Instincts

In a garden where socks find their mates,
And carrots hold secret debates.
The squirrels play chess with a knowing glance,
While tomatoes break out in a merry dance.

The weeds wear crowns like they're royalty now,
Claiming the throne, taking their bow.
The sunflowers giggle at ants that parade,
In a kingdom of greens, life's mischief displayed.

A Symphony of Survival

The daisies hum tunes of the lightest breeze,
While potatoes are plotting their big world tease.
Carrots in top hats, so posh and polite,
Invite all the bugs for a garden delight.

The radishes brag of their spicy flair,
While locusts just dance without a care.
A chorus of chirps fills the air with glee,
Even the weeds want to join in the spree.

The Echo of Life

In the lush underbrush, laughter takes root,
As frogs in bowties perform their sweet loot.
The daisies exchange gossip with sweet old trees,
And shadows point fingers at bumbles and bees.

The breeze whispers tales of the dozy crows,
While daisies complain of a rude garden hose.
Each leaf tells a story, each twig has a quirk,
Nature's punchline is all in the work.

Light Amidst the Layers

Beneath the soil, there's quite a rave,
Mice in tuxedos come out of their cave.
Potatoes in disco balls gleam in the dark,
While worms groove to life in their squiggle-mark.

The light filters down to play hide and seek,
With rays that tickle each leaf and each peak.
Cucumber sweaters offer hugs from the vine,
In this happy mess, the sun always shines.

Nourished by Shadows

In the garden of gloom, where the bunnies play,
I found a potato doing ballet.
It twisted and turned, oh what a sight,
Even the moon had to laugh at the night.

The weeds had a party, the ants brought the snacks,
While the cucumbers plotted their veggie attacks.
With sunlight to brag, they danced in the glow,
But shadows just chuckled, 'We love this show!'

Harmony of Hidden Life

A worm strummed a tune on a leaf for a chair,
While a grasshopper crooned 'Don't go anywhere!'
They had a duet, the mole sang bass,
While crickets provided a jig for the place.

In a world underfoot, where big toes don't roam,
Little critters threw parties, calling it home.
With laughter and music, they thrived underground,
Oh, to join that conga line, what joy would abound!

The Beauty Buried Deep

Beneath the soil where the funny things grow,
A carrot once claimed to be a pop star, you know.
With roots for fans and dirt in its hair,
It dreamt of the stage, with no one to scare.

The potatoes all giggled at the carrot's big dreams,
While the onions were plotting their tearful themes.
"Let's throw a surprise!" said the radish too bold,
"To celebrate beauty, even if it's just gold!"

Shades of Strength

There's strength in the shadows, so sturdy and sly,
Where sunflowers giggle at the ants as they fly.
With roots all entwined, they put on a show,
A dance of delight in the breezy flow.

The mushrooms were laughing, "We're quite the fun bunch!
Come join in our circle; we'll have a great lunch!"
Amidst all the ferns and the leaves that confound,
Life's quirkiest mysteries flourish around.

Deep in the Earth

Down in the soil where the worms like to play,
    Plants whisper secrets to lighten the day.
    Tiny roots giggle, they wiggle and twine,
      Sipping up nutrients, all of them dine.

Earthworms in jackets, they wiggle like kings,
    Throwing a party for all of their things.
    A dance in the dirt, the worms do a twirl,
While seeds make big wishes, oh what a whirl!

Luminous Growth

Sunshine's a prankster with rays so bright,
Tugging on leaves, giving them a fright.
Photosynthesis? Oh, what a show!
Chlorophyll giggles, 'Look how I glow!'

Ferns do a jig, they trade leafy tips,
With daisies who gossip and bloom with their quips.
The garden's a circus, with colors so loud,
All plants do a dance, they're growing so proud!

Anchored Blossoms

Roots play a game of tug-of-war,
They pull with a giggle, then stretch for more.
Blossoms above, swaying to a tune,
While bees hum a ditty, it's quite a boon.

They tell tales of the ground, oh what a hoot!
Of worms on a trek and a lost rubber boot.
All anchored below, they tell roots their tales,
A garden united, where humor prevails!

The Light Beneath

In tunnels so cozy, where light can't parade,
The critters get cozy, a fun little escapade.
They chuckle at sprouting green things up high,
'We're the foundation; they couldn't comply!'

Laughter erupts from the damp, earthy crew,
'We're the real stars, though they seek the view!'
While the sun gets the credit, they bask in the fun,
The underground party's just begun!

Glistening Roots

In the garden, worms do dance,
Their wiggles give the plants a chance.
With socks on heads and dirt on toes,
They throw a party, goodness knows!

The carrots wear their leafy hats,
While radishes chat with silly chats.
A beet quite proudly starts to sing,
In soil's embrace, they all are kings!

Rising from the Depths

Down below, the roots all scheme,
They plan a garden's wildest dream.
A broccoli knight with armor made,
    Starts a quest to serenade!

With onions' tears, they seek a muse,
A pumpkin queen in bright orange hues.
They laugh and joke, their spirits high,
    While meandering the earth, oh my!

The Heart of the Forest

Among the trees, a squirrel's jest,
He hid a nut, an acorn fest.
With giggles floating through the air,
He's quite the cheeky woodland heir!

The owls hoot riddle games all night,
While fireflies flash their crazy light.
In this embrace of bark and vine,
The woodland creatures sip on pine!

Hidden Glow

A mushroom pulled off quite a show,
With spots of red, it stole the glow.
A dance-off with a glowing bug,
Both twirling in their cozy rug!

In shadows deep, a lantern winked,
A glow that made the crickets think.
They chirp a tune, a playful night,
In nature's laughter, pure delight!

From Darkness to Dawn

In the shadows, a dance with the night,
A sunflower's giggle, a comical sight.
The moon winked once, then snored with glee,
While stars played tag 'round a funny old tree.

Oh, the dawn came in with a cat's sudden leap,
And slumbering creatures began to peep.
A rooster crowed as if he were king,
But tripped on a worm with a wild, silly swing.

The Strength of Hidden Beauty

Beneath the soil, a secret's delight,
A potato's dream of taking flight.
With eyes wide shut and a starchy grin,
It plots for a chance to dance and spin.

Oh, broccoli hides with a cloak of green,
Hoping to be the hip-hop queen.
While carrots shyly don their cool shades,
Rooting for styles that never quite fade.

Illuminated by Earth

Dirt makes the best blanket, snug and warm,
Worms tell jokes, creating quite the charm.
A tiny seed sprouted with a laugh,
Said, 'Watch out world, I'm here for the half!'

With sunbeams tickling, it bursts into cheer,
While daisies shake their petals like, 'Hear, hear!'
The soil high-fives a brave little sprout,
Together they giggle, without a doubt.

Flourish Where You Stand

A cactus decided to join in the fun,
Said, 'Who needs water? I'm still number one!'
With prickly vibes and a smile so bright,
It quipped to the blooms, 'You're all just polite!'

Meanwhile, a dandelion danced in the breeze,
'I'm fluffier than you,' it said with ease.
It blew its seeds, like confetti in air,
Leaving everyone else with a tinge of despair!

Emblems of Endurance

In the garden, we stand so tall,
Laughing at weeds and the fall.
With every storm, we sway and bend,
Oh, what a life, on us they depend!

The sun shines bright on our leafy heads,
While squirrels play twist and leap on their beds.
We giggle at clouds, so puffy and gray,
Singing our roots, 'Come join the fray!'

The Brilliance below

Down in the soil, a party's begun,
Worms wear their goggles, they're having such fun.
In the dark, we hold our grand dance,
With potatoes in tuxes, they prance and they prance!

The carrots hum tunes to the beet's jazzy groove,
While radishes pop with every smooth move.
Roots of all colors throw glitter and cheer,
Making the underground simply premier!

Tapestry of Tales

Gather 'round folks, we've stories to tell,
Of tangled vines and a plant circus swell.
The daisies are clowns, in outfits so bright,
While whispers of moles cause a comical fright.

The cucumber juggles, it slips and it falls,
Breaking the silence with giggles and calls.
As flowers exchange their tall tales and dreams,
Nature's a canvas of laughter and beams!

From Darkness, We Bloom

In shadows we linger, but don't be alarmed,
For even the quiet can dance, uncharmed.
With just a spark, we burst into light,
Telling the sun, 'Oh, what a delight!'

The flowers shout, 'Hey! Look at us shine!'
While cacti sing ballads of drinking good wine.
From gloom we arise, with jokes up our sleeves,
In gardens of laughter, let's fool all the leaves!

Vibrance from the Soil

In the garden where laughter grows,
Bright blooms laugh as the soft wind blows.
Worms wearing glasses, digging up the ground,
Squirrels dancing, oh what a sight found!

A gnome with a hat, far too large to wear,
Tells tales of radishes with flair and care.
Petunias giggle as they sway and twirl,
While bees argue over their honeyed world.

Nourished by Shadows

In the corners where sunlight hesitates,
Grow plants that debate their dinner plates.
A cactus confesses it's scared of the rain,
While mushrooms giggle, "Lettuce go again!"

The shadows all whisper behind the tall trees,
"Who needs sunshine? We've got plenty of cheese!"
A tomato blushes, feeling so shy,
While the parsley dances, too proud to comply.

Flourishing Foundations

Roots converse over a cup of tea,
Sharing gossip, so wild and free.
One says, "I can't, my leaves are too wide!"
The other retorts, "Come on, let's ride!"

They plot to grow taller than the fence,
With dreams of a wall, such great expense.
The daisies are snickering, fully amused,
At the antics of plants who refuse to be bruised.

Glimmers in the Underground

Deep down where the secrets softly thrive,
Worms write stories that come alive.
A potato laughs, "I'm the true spud king!"
While radishes boast about the joy they bring.

They throw a party with snacks all around,
Underground music with no ear-splitting sound.
The moles play their tunes, beats heavy with funk,
While roots wiggle and twist, all lively and sunk.

Stem and Starlight

In my garden, veggies dance,
With radishes in funny pants.
Tomatoes giggle, squash rolls by,
As beans compete to touch the sky.

Sunflowers wear the brightest hats,
Swinging to tunes of playful chats.
Carrots crack jokes from underground,
While mushrooms giggle all around.

Bees buzz in a silly hive,
In their tiny world, they thrive.
With every bloom, there's laughter there,
In this garden, joy's the air.

Blossoms of Resilience

Petunias wear a vibrant grin,
While daisies waltz with a spin.
Roses tell tales of daring feats,
As violets churn out sweet beats.

Each flower boasts a funny trait,
Like dandelions who love to skate.
They spin and twirl with such delight,
As clouds all giggle, fluffy and white.

Sunshine tickles every bloom,
A garden party, everyone's in tune.
These blossoms know how to have fun,
In their playful, colorful run.

Overcoming the Grime

A weed in sneakers gives a cheer,
With mud-covered shoes, it has no fear.
While dirt may cling, it struts with pride,
Singing loud—a wild joyride!

Worms wear scarves made of the soil,
As snails parade with their shiny toil.
Through grime and muck, they dance and sway,
Turning the mess into a play.

Rain drops laugh as they make a splash,
Turning dull days into a bash.
Even puddles join the scheme,
In this quirky, globby dream.

Spirals of Existence

Twisted vines give a goofy wink,
While ivy plays hide and seek with stink.
Every curl holds a silly tune,
In this spiral, joy finds room.

A snail sings softly on the path,
Calculating its next math.
With a flip and a twirl it goes,
Chasing shadows while it grows.

In tangled twists, the world aligns,
Dancing with absurd old designs.
Here in the chaos, fun abounds,
As life spins circles and makes sounds.

The Pulse of Nature

In the garden of giggles and glee,
Plants whisper secrets, oh so carefree.
A busy bee trips, lands on my shoe,
Buzzing apologies, what else can it do?

The petunias laugh, petals in a whirl,
Tulips tell jokes, sending the bees in a twirl.
The worms throw a party beneath the ground,
With roots as their DJ, the best beats around!

Every leaf dances, sways side to side,
Even the thorns wear a prickly slide.
Nature's the maestro, conducting the fun,
In this uproarious symphony, there's laughter for everyone.

So let's take a stroll in the sunny embrace,
Join in the silliness, find your own space.
The pulse of nature, filled with mirth,
Who knew the garden could entertain such worth?

Flourish in the Fray

In a pot of chaos, plants take their stand,
Trying to outgrow each other, it's a land!
Succulents are sassy, cacti act tough,
But once they get together, they laugh till they huff.

Herbs hold a gossip, with basil so bold,
Thyme adds the spice, the stories unfold.
Rosemary winks, for it knows all the tea,
This riotous garden is wild and carefree.

Grass blades are tickled by footfalls near,
While flowers wear petals to celebrate cheer.
The daisies do cartwheels, all dressed in white,
In this fray of flora, everything feels light.

So join in the tomfoolery, watch them play,
With roots in the ground, they won't drift away.
In this playful bungle, nature's the muse,
Flourish in the fray; we've nothing to lose!

Depths of Delight

Down in the soil where the secrets lie,
Earthworms enjoy mud pies, oh my!
With shovels and forks, we delve and dig,
Nature plays hide and seek, it's quite a gig!

Deep in those depths, the fungi hold court,
Throwing a feast with a mushroom report.
The daisies sneak peeks, making faces so bold,
While the snails carry houses, treasures of old.

Wiggly roots wiggle, dance in the muck,
With every big gust, they just smile and chuck.
In the depths of the garden, fun never ends,
With laughter and joy, there's no need to pretend.

So join in the digging, a treasure to find,
In the world underground, with laughter aligned.
From the grit grows the giggles, a natural sight,
In these depths of delight, all worries take flight!

The Light Beneath

Beneath the surface, where mischief brews,
The critters are plotting, sharing their views.
Worms are the comedians, telling bad puns,
And roots crack up over their daily runs.

In the cool dark, they twist and they turn,
Trying to dance, though feeling concern.
Fungi flash lights like disco balls bright,
Creating a raucous end to the night.

The soil's alive, with crackles and cheer,
Every creature's laughing, come gather near.
The ladybugs giggle, the beetles all clap,
In this underground rave, they've set quite the trap!

So if you should wander where sunlight can't seep,
Remember the humor that lies beneath deep.
With silliness sprouting and joy in full view,
The light beneath shines, forever anew.

Flourishing in Shadows

In the garden of the quirky, big feet abound,
Where carrots wear sunglasses, and greens dance around.
Tomatoes gossip softly, all covered in rain,
While eggplants act sassy, mischief in their grain.

A sunflower with a wink, leans over to tease,
'Why do cucumbers blush? They're just trying to freeze!'
Bees wear tiny hats, buzzing jokes on the go,
As radishes roll laughter, putting on a show.

The shadows stretch longer as the day starts to fade,
Yet in this sneaky garden, no one's ever afraid.
With humor as fertilizer, they grow without fright,
Creating giggles and chuckles in the soft, fading light.

Beneath the Canopy

Underneath the tall trees, a picnic unfolds,
With squirrels as the guests, each wearing their gold.
They nibble on acorns while sharing their tales,
Of misadventures chasing after their tails.

Beneath the huge leaves, laughter fills the air,
As chipmunks tell jokes from their comfy chair.
A frog in a bow tie shows off with glee,
'Why did the mushroom always get invited? It's a fun guy, you see!'

The shadows dance playfully, where mischief resides,
As raccoons swap secrets, no need to divide.
In this lively gathering, no room for a frown,
Just giggles and cheer, beneath leafy towns.

Glimmering Grace

In the morning dew, the daisies prance,
With bees doing tango, a buzzing romance.
Butterflies wear ruffles and sashay on by,
While ants are the dancers, with their tiny bow ties.

A goldfish takes a stroll in its watery sphere,
Winking at the lotus, 'You shine bright, my dear!'
As frogs croak the beats, the pond comes alive,
With laughter and splashes as everyone dives.

Light flickers like starlight on petals that sway,
While dragonflies giggle and flit all the day.
In this radiant chaos, where silliness thrives,
Joy glimmers like sunshine, making all come alive!

Anchored in Time

In a garden of time where the past loves to play,
An old gnome tells stories of skies turning gray.
With a wink and a chuckle, he spins out the lore,
Of the antics of plants when they first hit the floor.

The flowers remember how wild the breeze blew,
When daisies wore bell-bottoms, and violets grew too.
Grasshoppers tap danced on the edge of a clue,
While worms cheered them on in a colorful hue.

Underneath the wise oak, the moments stand still,
As squirrels shift their plans with a sprinkle of thrill.
Time holds a giggle, a wink, and a jest,
In this garden of memory, it's always the best.

Nature's Silent Symphony

In the woods where squirrels dance,
Leaves play hide and seek by chance,
The birds debate who sings the best,
While crickets chirp, they never rest.

Bamboo's gossip tickles the air,
Trees gossip louder, but who would care?
A bunny winks in sunlight's glare,
Nature's jesters, always fair!

The wind hums softly, tunes divine,
Raccoons debate, 'What's your sign?'
A flower chuckles in the breeze,
While ants parade, 'Look at us, please!'

Life's a giggle, a merry jest,
In nature's arms, we jest and rest.
Every creature has their role,
In this grand show, they share their soul.

Beneath the Surface

Underneath where mudworms plot,
Laughter bubbles in a secret spot.
Turtles argue who's got the best shell,
While catfish giggle, 'We know it well!'

The minnows dance, a tiny prance,
While algae's got a groovy stance.
Octopus tells the best tall tales,
While seahorses don their tiny veils.

Crustaceans grumble, 'It's not fair!'
As starfish lounge without a care.
The seaweed sways to the beat,
Beneath the waves, life's a treat.

And down below, in twilight's glee,
For every critic, there's a spree.
In watery depths, we're all afloat,
With bubbles bursting, let's take note!

A Tapestry of Life

In gardens where the colors clash,
Bees get busy, making a splash.
Sunflowers giggle, reaching high,
While daisies whisper, 'Why so shy?'

A ladybug dons her polka dots,
Rabbits nibble on their favorite spots.
While worms roll out the welcome mat,
The earth still laughs, 'How about that?'

Butterflies flutter in a parade,
Flowers wink, 'We've got it made!'
A honeybee holds court, so wise,
As bugs perform their funny tries.

Life spins on in vibrant hues,
Nature's stage with endless views.
Each petal tickles, every leaf beams,
In this canvas, nothing's as it seems.

Whispering Roots

In the ground where secrets lie,
Roots hold stories, oh my, oh my!
Caterpillars plot their grand escape,
While moles giggle, sharing some grape.

The fungi throw a party, so bold,
Mushrooms whisper secrets untold.

Life Underground

In the soil, where the critters play,
Worms dance around, come what may.
Mice throw parties, oh what a sight,
With dancing roots, they groove all night.

One ant lost his map, oh what a mess,
He found a potato, claimed it his dress.
They all laughed at his starchy delight,
While snails took laps; pure marathon fright.

The groundhogs gossip, what's brewing today?
Squirrels just yell, 'Get out of my way!'
In a world beneath, quirky and spry,
They plot grand adventures beneath the sky.

Each day a new tale of laughter and cheer,
In this underground party, all friends appear.
So if you dig deep, don't fear what you find,
Just remember, above, it's all in your mind.

The Color of Connection

Inhaling colors from roots below,
Where grass wears sneakers and flowers glow.
Beetles in shades of electric green,
Swapping their gossip like it's routine.

A daisy's pink, a tulip's red,
They paint the soil, where dreams are fed.
But one purple sprout thought he was blue,
Claimed he was the sky, with a cosmic view.

Caterpillars boast, 'Oh, we're trendy today!'
Twirling in shades of the rainbow play.
They spin silk threads like a fashion spree,
But forget it's a cocoon; they're late for tea!

So cheers to the colors that dance in the earth,
Celebrating friendship, giving it worth.
In this vibrant party, we twirl and we sway,
With roots intertwined, there's always a way.

Awe of the Deep

Down in the depths where the laughter is loud,
Live fish in tuxedos, feeling so proud.
They throw seaweed balls, everyone shares,
With a reef of friends, no one compares.

Crabs pinch playfully, 'Tag! You're it!'
While octopuses juggle, not one little bit.
Anemones giggle, with tentacles spread,
As the clownfish parade, that's their bedspread.

Turtles take selfies with sea urchin pals,
Shouting, 'We look great!' amid laughter and jowls.
But the dolphin's too vain, won't swim in the frame,
'My fin's not up to par, what a shame!'

So deep in the blue, where the joy's never cheap,
Even the krill join in, taking a leap.
With friendship and laughter, beneath waves they play,
Underwater antics at the end of the day.

Shining Through the Ground

Up from the dirt, a sprout starts to show,
With a leafy grin, saying, 'Hello!'
But wait, what's this? A worm pops his head,
'You're blocking my view! Just take it instead!'

The daffodils laugh, with their bright sunny face,
'We're waving to sunbeams, come join the race!'
But a stubborn weed claims the best plot of land,
'You can't take my space, just don't make a stand.'

A mushroom pipes up, 'I'll throw you a party!
With dances and snacks, it'll be super hearty!'
But the gophers all giggle, building a maze,
'A party underground? Now that'll amaze!'

So the garden erupts with laughter and zeal,
With roots intertwined, they all share a meal.
Through soil and sun, they find happy ground,
In a world full of humor, life laughs all around.

Life in the Darkness

In the shadows, I dance with delight,
Hiding from monsters, wearing a light.
My socks are unmatched, a fashion faux pas,
But who needs style when you're the star?

The fridge is a treasure, where snacks laugh and play,
I'm the brave knight, on a quest for the whey.
With each midnight raid, I fight off my fate,
With a cookie in hand, I feel really great.

The curtains are drawn, the whispers rejoice,
In a room full of silence, I hear my own voice.
I stumble on shoes, a pitiful trip,
But it's all part of the comedy script.

So here's to the night, wild and profound,
Where giggles erupt in the dark all around.
Life may be messy, but I'm dressed with a grin,
In this grand hall of chaos, I just can't help win!

Echoes of the Ancient

In caveman times, I'd be a great chief,
Riding my mammoth, oh what a belief!
But here in the now, I trip on my feet,
Searching for wisdom, in the kitchen I eat.

With sassy cavemen explaining it all,
I'm still reading scrolls that come from the mall.
They say, "Stay grounded!" while I soar like a kite,
Wondering what's ancient behind this old light.

I dance like a dodo, with great silly flair,
Spinning on stones with wild, crazy hair.
Laughter in eons, echoing through,
Past tribes would be rolling, just watching me too.

From fossils to fads, we're all here to jest,
Life's one grand stage, and I'm just a guest.
With ancient ambitions, I'm stuck in this age,
But painting my life on a humorous page!

Glistening Through Grit

When life gets tough, I sprinkle some flair,
In mud pies and laughter, there's magic to share.
So what if I tumble in dirt, face full of grime,
I'll emerge with a sparkle, oh so sublime!

Like butter on toast, I slip through the day,
With a grin that's contagious, come join in the play!
Fallen and bruised, but with a silly song,
I'll dance through the chaos, where I belong.

The world can be rough, like a giant who sneezes,
Yet I'll shine like the stars, finding joy in the breezes.
With grit in my heart and a wink in my eye,
I'll navigate life like a pizza pie!

So here's to the struggles, and the jokes that we share,
With laughter and kindness, life's not so unfair.
Through trial and mischief, I'll twirl and I'll spin,
Unyielding and bright, let the fun times begin!

The Silent Awakening

In the stillness of morn, I rise like a cake,
With a stretch and a yawn, there's no chance I'll fake.
The world starts to wake with the buzz and the chirp,
But I'm still in my jammies, a glorious slurp.

Coffee in hand, I'm a wizard of beans,
Conjuring magic with my breakfast machine.
While others jump up, all crisp and adult,
I'm channeling sloth; it's my favorite default.

The sun peeks in cautiously, whispering cheer,
But I'm entangled in sheets, with no reason to fear.
I laugh with the shadows, a giggly parade,
In my sleepy kingdom, where dreams never fade.

So let them all hurry, with their busy parade,
I'm mastering stillness, a unique escapade.
With joy in the quiet, I learn to unwind,
In this silent awakening, pure fun's what I find!

Where Starlight Meets the Soil

Under the stars, plants do a dance,
Wiggling their leaves, like they've got a chance.
Giggling roots whisper secrets at night,
While moonbeams chuckle—what a funny sight!

In the garden, gnomes hold a debate,
Who's the tallest? They each contemplate.
With a wink, a sunflower joins the brawl,
Saying, 'I grow taller than all of y'all!'

The daisies snicker, all wearing their crowns,
Making fun of the shy little frowns.
Meanwhile, the weeds just lie there and chill,
Claiming they're the best, with time to kill!

Beneath twinkling skies, the fun will not quit,
Plants and the stars snicker, never do sit.
With roots in the dirt and heads in the air,
They laugh and they grow, without a care!

Thriving in Stillness

In the quiet of dusk, all the critters yawn,
While the grand old oak keeps groaning till dawn.
Its branches sway lightly, whispering tales,
Of squirrels who swing from the backs of snales!

The moss plays it cool, like a green fuzzy hat,
Boasting 'I'm the cushion; where's everyone at?'
With a chuckle it watches as shadows roam near,
All the while grinning without any fear!

A snail pulls a face, as it slithers on by,
'Are you sure it's just me? Or am I flying high?'
The tree starts to giggle, shaking its leaves,
'This party's a blast, truth be told, who believes?'

So in stillness they bloom, each creature with flair,
Turning whispers and laughter into a rare air.
Under the moon's gaze, all troubles take flight,
In the sacred calm, they shimmer with delight!

From Depths to Light

Down in the earth where the worms like to play,
The roots tell a joke about the sun's silly rays.
They wiggle and giggle, with mud on their cheek,
'Hey, what do we owe to that light up there peak?'

The tulips peek up, with colors so bright,
'Why do we blossom if we fear the night?'
A daffodil chimes in, with sass and delight,
'Because after the rain, we shine oh so bright!'

As the daisies debate if they're bold or shy,
The thistles roll 'round, like 'Oh me, oh my!'
In the sunlight's embrace, they chatter and muse,
Finding humor in the darkness that they refuse.

So underground giggles blend with the day,
From roots to the sky, they laugh in their way.
In the dance of the dirt and beams from above,
Everyone's buzzing with laughter and love!

Fortitude in Bloom

Behold the brave blooms pushing through stone,
In a fight for their chance, despite being alone.
With a wink, a dandelion challenges fate,
Saying, 'I'm just here to be great, yeah mate!'

Petunias parade in their vibrant attire,
Razzle-dazzling bees as if they're on fire.
'Oh darling,' says Rose with a twirl and a sigh,
'We're starting a rumor—let's spread it up high!'

Lilies laugh loud, in their posh little way,
'Thanks to our roots, we're here to stay!'
The garden erupts in a fit of delight,
With every petal pointing at the sun's light.

From cracks in the pavement, to heights of the sky,
These flowers keep giggling as clouds drift on by.
It's a vortex of fun where resilience can bloom,
Finding joy every step in their quest to consume!

Enchantment of the Enigma

In a garden of whispers, plants wear a grin,
The daisies gossip while the tulips spin.
I asked the roses, with petals so bright,
'Tell me your secrets, or I'll steal your light!'

The carrots chuckled, so snug underground,
While the onions cried, for they had no sound.
The beans had a party, swinging in the breeze,
Calling the peas, 'Come join us, if you please!'

With ferns as the backdrop, so lush and so green,
The hedgehogs arrived, wearing hats they had seen.
They danced with the bugs, to a tune made of hums,
Creating a chaos, oh, the joy that it sums!

As twilight descended, the fun did not cease,
The crickets played marbles beneath the leaf trees.
In the garden of laughter, all creatures unite,
Under stars that giggle, what a silly night!

Legacy of the Undergrowth

Beneath the tall trees, a riddle unfolds,
With critters exchanging the tales that they've told.
The frogs croak sonnets, while lizards break dance,
A ruckus of laughter, oh what a funny chance!

The mushrooms are winking, all dressed up in spots,
While ants in their tuxedos pull off daring plots.
'Hey, Mr. Snail, can you pick up the pace?'
'Not on your life! I'm just winning this race!'

In shadows they gather; the whispers grow wide,
As hedgehogs exchange jokes, with porcupines snide.
A dialogue on thorns, oh, what a fine mess,
When the bramble makes jokes, it's simply the best!

And as the sun sets, with a flick of a tail,
All critters unite in a musical wail.
The legacy thrives where the laughter rings clear,
In the depth of the forest, it's silly, my dear!

Conversations in the Dark

At midnight's cool cloak, the shadows convene,
The owls spin tall tales, oh what a routine.
They hoot about rabbits and their silly schemes,
In the moonlight they flourish, creating wild dreams!

The hedgehogs in huddles share how they can't roll,
While fireflies plan dances, twinkling in soul.
A wise old tortoise chimes in with wise cracks,
'Take it slow, little friends, or you'll end up in snacks!'

The stars are their audience, shimmering bright,
As the critters throw punches, in laughter and fright.
With every good joke, there's a rustle nearby,
A raccoon, quite cheeky, just came to the spy!

As daylight tiptoes, those murmurs now fade,
Still echoing softly, the light in their shades.
In conversations of night, silly tales leave a mark,
Where laughter is found in the depths of the dark!

Starters of Seasons

When spring pops up, like a kid in the sun,
The flowers start popping, each race has begun.
The daisies are bragging, 'We're the best of the bunch!'
While tulips just roll their eyes, thinking 'Not in a punch!'

When summer rolls in with its bright, silly vibes,
The bees buzz around like they're actors in jibes.
A picnic is forming; ants bring the soup,
'Careful now, daisies, you might just get stooped!'

Then autumn arrives with a rustle of leaves,
Where pumpkins wear hats, and the scarecrow believes.
They gather for stories on chilly starry nights,
In a quilt made of laughter, oh what fun it ignites!

Winter's the finale, all snowy and cold,
The squirrels play pranks, oh they're brazen and bold.
They slide on the ice, with a wobble, a cheer,
In a season where giggles bring warmth close and near!

Awakening in the Abyss

In the depths where shadows play,
Chasing sleep has gone astray.
A snail in slippers takes a stroll,
Dreams of pizza, that's the goal.

The coffee pot sings a tune,
While I dance like a buffoon.
A sock puppet joins the fun,
Who knew mornings weighed a ton?

A cat debates with a chair,
Shakes its head like it don't care.
I trip on thoughts, they're everywhere,
Making breakfast? Beware, beware!

Finally, I rise, a burst of cheer,
Sipping joy, not that old fear.
The abyss laughs, "Isn't this neat?"
A shining start, can't be beat!

Dance Amongst Roots

Twisting limbs in soil's embrace,
That worm thinks it's in a race.
A squirrel shows off acorn tricks,
While ants are planning political picks.

Leafy hats and wiggly shoes,
Each root a friend I can't refuse.
We shimmy and shake in the sun,
Who knew choreography was this fun?

The breeze giggles, a song so spry,
My branches wave, oh me, oh my!
Nature's party, a riotous bash,
Even the stones have learned to dash!

So dance with fungi or do a jig,
Join hands with the bugs, let's dance big!
A blend of laughter, joy, and grace,
In this forest, we found our place.

Leaning Through the Gloom

In shadows where the odd things creep,
I fumble, tumble, and God, I leap!
With a hairpin twist, and a wild shout,
What was that? A shadow—oh, there's no doubt!

Mushrooms whisper as I pass,
"Don't trip on daisies, that's so brass!"
A toad sits in a little chair,
Guzzling soda, without a care.

I lean and sway, hope for a breeze,
Vines sneak in, part of the tease.
Falling leaves do a waltz with glee,
Is this nature or a circus spree?

So, let's toast to the gloomy nights,
When the oddest creatures make it right.
Laugh in the fog, it's quite the sight—
Dancing through darkness, a sheer delight!

Veins of Vitality

Bouncing beetles in a wild race,
With a grin that lights the place.
I think they're training for the big show,
The Olympic games of the insect flow.

A butterfly farts, oh what a sound!
It leaves all the blooms spinning round.
Honeybees buzz with gossip in flight,
"Did you see the grasshopper's new highlight?"

Roots tickle each other below,
An underground party, don't you know?
They share secrets, like "Why's the grass blue?"
Nature chuckles, it's ancient and true.

So lift your glass and shout with glee,
For every sapling, every tree.
In this lively realm, we're never flat,
Embrace the quirkiness, imagine that!

Splashes of the Subterranean

Down below where gnomes do play,
They splash in mud—what a funny day!
With leafy hats and acorn shoes,
They dance and giggle, sing the blues.

Worms join in with silken curls,
They twirl around, such silly swirls!
In their party, no roots can hide,
Just fun and laughter, side by side.

Fungi wear hats, mushrooms stand tall,
A shroomy dance is fun for all.
With the turn of the earth, they store their cheer,
To pop up and party once spring is here!

So raise your glass for the underground crew,
Celebrating life—potato soup, too!
With soil deep, their jokes never fade,
In the depths of the dirt, a grand charade!

Cherished Below

Among the roots, a rabbit sneezes,
Carrots giggle, oh! It never ceases.
They tell long tales of underground fun,
While ants march by, on their moonlit run.

Old trees whisper secrets quite bizarre,
They discuss the latest gossip from afar.
"Did you hear of that flower who danced?
She twirled and spun, it left us entranced!"

The moles throw a party with cake made of mud,
With jellied worms, isn't that quite a dud?
Yet everyone chuckles, what a wild spread,
As radishes roar, "Let's dance instead!"

So raise a toast to the roots' special crew,
In their soil shower, they celebrate you!
In the quiet dark, each giggle is vast,
For the bond of the earth is such a blast!

Essence of the Earth

Deep in the dirt, a party unfolds,
Where the laughter of potatoes is worth more than gold.
They tell silly jokes, cackle with glee,
As earthworms wiggle their way to the spree.

A wise old tree croaks a pun every hour,
"Life's like a root—full of twists and power!"
With leaves that rustle, they cheer and conspire,
To tickle the soil with jokes that inspire.

The beetles unite for their fancy ball,
Dressed up in soil with no worries at all.
They dance on the grasses, low to the ground,
In this earthy realm, pure delight must abound!

So here's to the merry, the quirky and loud,
To the essence of nature, so unique and proud.
With giggles and roots intertwined in the mirth,
Among echoes of life, we cherish the earth!

Timeless Growth

Beneath the sky, where the shadows play,
The sprouts tell jokes at the end of the day.
A sunflower sings, "Come dance with me!
We'll twirl till dawn, just wait and see!"

With carrots in tutus and radishes bright,
They laugh at the moon in the soft night light.
Chubby potatoes roll, laughing round,
In the soil's embrace, good humor is found.

A tiny acorn dreams of a grand old oak,
Whispering, "Trust me, I'm no funny joke!"
Though the roots intertwine and the winds may blow,
The best laughs are shared in the dirt below.

So here's to the joy that life can bestow,
In gardens of laughter, we endlessly grow.
With nature's quirks, our hearts take flight,
In the timeless embrace of day and night!

The Hidden Grace.

In a garden where veggies all prance,
A potato just thought it could dance.
With a shimmy and shake,
It gave us a break,
And turned the whole harvest to chance.

The carrots wore shades, looking cool,
While radishes ruled the vegetable school.
They chuckled and teased,
As they formed a big freeze,
And painted the lettuce a drool.

The onions kept crying, so loud,
While beets dressed up, feeling so proud.
They twirled for the bees,
With flashy old knees,
Creating a side-salad crowd!

In this veggie affair, such delight,
Even turnips joined in for the night.
With costumes and cheer,
The harvest felt near,
As laughter bloomed under moonlight.

Deep in the Earth.

Beneath the crust, where the critters do slide,
Worms throw a party with nature as guide.
They dance with the rocks,
In their muddy old socks,
And giggle when moles try to hide.

A beetle's looking for a mate,
But tripping on roots proves quite fate.
He slips with a plop,
But refuses to stop,
Declaring his dance is first-rate!

The fungi are wild, playing tricks,
As they moldy-mold out at their fix.
With spore confetti,
They celebrate ready,
For mischief in soils, like old flicks.

In this underground realm, oh so deep,
They giggle and laugh when they sleep.
With a hint of surprise,
They dream in disguise,
As shadows above start to creep.

Luminescence from Within.

In a patch where the seedlings all gleam,
A glowworm was caught in a dream.
He wished he could fly,
Until a bee buzzed by,
And said, 'You, my friend, are supreme!'

The daisies, they giggled with glee,
As the worm tried to sip on his tea.
He spilled in a whirl,
The results made him twirl,
And made such a mess, oh dear me!

The tomatoes were blushing with pride,
As they watched the worm slip and slide.
"A glowworm can bop,
With a wiggle and hop,
When he eats all the snacks we provide!"

Beneath the stars, they all shared a toast,
To the worm and the fun he'd engross.
With laughter that shone,
Their friendship was known,
In their leafy old garden cornered close.

Embracing the Soil.

A cactus held hands with a spud,
Saying, 'Let's dance in a muddy old flood!'
They waltzed with a pie,
Underneath the vast sky,
As laughter bounced off every bud.

The petals were flapping, quite proud,
While clouds gathered round as a crowd.
They clapped with delight,
'We'll dance through the night!'
As the roots cheered, 'Together we're loud!'

A gopher popped up, thought he could sing,
But the flowers just laughed at his bling.
With soil on his nose,
He struck a pose,
And earned himself quite the good ring.

As night's curtain fell, oh what a sight,
The garden was glowing with light.
The critters all cheered,
As joy reappeared,
In the soil, all together, so bright!

Brilliance of the Buried

Beneath the soil, I tell you right,
Worms throw parties, what a sight!
Tangles and twirls in earthy delight,
With mushrooms dancing under the moonlight.

Roots holding hands in a veggie ballet,
Carrots gossip in the roots all day.
Potatoes chuckle at the sunlight's ray,
While radishes argue, "You're in my way!"

Beneath our feet, a hootenanny grows,
Where beet and turnip share silly prose.
Down here, everyone gladly knows,
The dirt is where the fun really flows.

So next time you walk on that patch of green,
Remember the shenanigans seldom seen.
Underneath the grass, it's a lively scene,
With laughter sprouting in the unseen machine.

Vibrations of the Understory

In layers deep where shadows play,
Frogs croak tunes, hip-hop ballet.
Crickets chirp in a jazzy sway,
While mushrooms groove to the earth's ballet.

Roots wiggle like they're dancing bold,
The ferns are spinning stories untold.
Even the soil has rhythm, behold!
In the underground club, fun never gets old.

Squirrels drop beats, and the mice clap along,
The beetles' band plays a silly song.
Every critter joins in, it's never wrong,
In the understory, where all feel strong.

So when you think of the things that creep,
Remember the parties that never sleep.
In the dark, there's fun more than we can keep,
Life beneath us is the universe's peep.

Sunlight Through the Leaves

Up above, those leaves do sway,
Sunbeams tickle in a playful way.
The branches giggle, come out and play,
As squirrels zip by in a bright display.

Light drips down like lemonade sweet,
Bouncing off flowers to a shiny beat.
The petals laugh as critters greet,
In a sunlit warm embrace, what a treat!

The shade makes a cooler, sneaky spot,
Where yo-yos hang, and jokes get hot.
Under the canopy, a game is caught,
It's a leafy maze—who's found what?

So step beneath that glorious tree,
Join the party, come dance with glee.
In the sunlight's glow, let spirits be free,
As laughter unfurls in nature's decree.

Whispers of the Ground

Listen close, can you hear the cheer?
The dirt has secrets, they're quite near.
With giggles of roots, every footstep clear,
In soil's soft voice, joy is sincere.

Ants swap stories of their daily grind,
While grubs munch snacks, and love is blind.
Under the surface, jokes are designed,
And laughter rumbles, one of a kind.

Beneath the grass, a ticklish breeze,
Makes dandelions dance with ease.
With every step, the underground teases,
Join the fun, oh, if you please.

So if you wander, just take a seat,
In nature's laughter, life's bittersweet.
From whispers on the ground, joy can't be beat,
Come share a giggle, a tasty treat.

Luminaries of the Undergrowth

In the shadows where mushrooms dance,
Beneath the ferns, they take a chance.
With every giggle of a tiny sprout,
They plot to turn the garden out!

Worms parade in hats made of leaves,
Telling tales of autumn eves.
A snail's joke is slow as molasses,
Yet in the soil, it truly passes!

The ants throw parties, quite the affair,
With crumbs as confetti, flying everywhere!
'Let's boogie, my friends,' a crow shouts loud,
As the beetles form a conga line proud.

In the mud, the frogs sing off-key,
Accidentally stepping on a bee!
Oh, the joy beneath nature's cover,
Where chaos reigns, but all is lover.

The Heartbeat of Flora

In a garden where daisies eavesdrop,
Tulips gossip without a prob.
Petunias snicker at the tall sunflowers,
'Your hair's in bloom!' they tease for hours.

Bees buzz by with a tune so sweet,
While ladybugs shuffle on tiny feet.
A moth trips over the morning dew,
'Oops, excuse me!'—with a flair too.

Vines are twining, tangled, and spry,
Playing twister beneath the sky.
'One hand on pink, oh what a laugh!'
And the thorns sharp giggle, 'Cry, if you must!'

In the soil, the roots high-five,
To make sure that they're all alive.
Nature's humor, playful and free,
Brings joy to all, including me!

Underneath the Canopy

Under trees, where squirrels conspire,
They discuss nuts, and dreams to inspire.
'Let's build a fort,' one whispers low,
While a chipmunk chimes, 'I'm in the know!'

The shadows play tricks on the dandelion,
Who believes the sprout can be a lion!
He roars softly, a fluffy faux king,
While the daisies laugh at his goofy fling.

A rake snickers, as he watches the scene,
Leaves distracted by a butterfly's sheen.
'You've got to focus, get in the game!'
But the ladybugs just know how to tame.

In a world of giggles and playful delight,
The critters frolic from morning to night.
With stories and laughter living in spree,
Underneath the trees, they want to be!

Soft Resurgence

When spring arrives, the flowers leap,
All buzzing about—no time for sleep.
'Let's throw a bash for the sun's warm rays!'
'Pastries of pollen!' the bee proudly plays.

The earth cracks jokes, a delightful scene,
With worms wriggling in an earthy routine.
'What did the seed say to the rain?'
'You make me sprout, it's such a gain!'

Bubbles of laughter rise with the dew,
As daisies debate who'll wear the best hue.
'Your petals are nice, but mine can twirl!'
With every petal, they happily swirl.

In a riot of colors, a kaleidoscope spreads,
Fun erupts from the roots to the heads.
A symphony of giggles, nature's ballet,
Dancing together—a fanciful display!

Glowy Roots

In the garden, worms do dance,
Jazzing it up with a chance.
Sunshine giggles, plants do sway,
Under the ground, it's a wild ballet.

Carrots hide from the busy bee,
"Please don't pull me!" they plead with glee.
Tomatoes chuckle, ripe and round,
"Here's your salad!" they sing, proud sound.

Emerging from Complexity

Beneath a pile of tangled roots,
Lay some funky, dancing shoots.
They peek out with a quirky grin,
Saying, "Let the garden party begin!"

Sideways grow a potato or two,
Waving frantically like, "Hey, what's new?"
Complex life, a circus show,
With laughing leaves putting on a glow.

Splendor in the Shadows

In the dark, where the critters play,
A mysterious party, hip-hip-hooray!
Mushrooms wiggle, they start to groove,
Under moonlight, they've got the move.

Sneaky ferns and shifty moss,
Whispering secrets, they're the boss.
"Shhh! Keep it down!" they softly tease,
Glow-in-the-dark, at ease with the breeze!

Layers of Luminescence

In a cake of soil, flavors great,
Each layer hiding a fun-filled fate.
Carrot sprinkles and radish cream,
A veggie dessert that makes you beam!

Roots beneath like jellybeans,
Brightening up the dullest scenes.
With each bite comes a burst of cheer,
Growing giggles, loud and clear!

Revival from Below

In the ground, I wiggle and squirm,
With dirt on my face, oh how I squirm!
Up I pop with a style so grand,
Announcing my presence like a marching band!

The sun gives me high fives and rays,
While the worms below dance in a haze.
Life's a party when you're stuck in the muck,
And who knew soggy soil could be so pluck?

I wear leaves like crowns, it's quite a sight,
With bugs as my entourage, oh what a delight!
Roots style their moves, both humble and sleek,
While I showcase my charm - it's peak physique!

With laughter, I grow, what a merry affair,
Just a little plant with dreams to spare.
I sway and I wave in the breeze without care,
Strutting my stuff, with a flair oh so rare!

The Beauty of Resilience

Through cracks in concrete, I find my way,
A stubborn sprout, come what may.
Though storms may batter and winds may sway,
I laugh at danger, I'll never decay!

My petals shine bright, though I'm sometimes small,
With a quirky dance and a twirl in the fall.
I wear my struggle like a sparkle hat,
Each raindrop a friend, what do you think of that?

Roots digging deep, oh what a plot twist,
In a world made of bricks, you get the gist.
Waving to cars, as they drive on by,
"Hey, look at me!" I yell with a sigh.

So here's to the moments that make us stand tall,
Even when life wants us to crawl.
Funny how growth blooms from the craziest scenes,
Like a flower that giggles in its wrinkly jeans!

Caught Between Elements

In the battle of rain against the sun,
I'm the referee, just trying to have fun.
Lightning says 'zap!' while thunder brings cheers,
I sway in the chaos, dismissing my fears!

Nature's a circus, and here I am,
Juggling the winds with a wink and a jam.
Saltwater air meets fresh mountain spritz,
What a mix! Like my plant-based blitz!

With clouds overhead, I put on a show,
Dancing to breezes as I wiggle below.
I've got my roots tied to the soil so nice,
While a raindrop lands, I giggle - that's my advice!

Caught in the fun of this weather parade,
I laugh and I bloom, my worries allayed.
So let's share a chuckle, no matter the storm,
Crazy little sprout, breaking every norm!

Spirit of the Soil

Oh soil, you glorious gooey delight,
Home to the critters that dance in the night.
With mud on my face, I embrace the grub,
In the party of flora, I'm the funky shrub!

The ladybugs laugh as they skitter around,
They've all got my back, my squad is profound.
Earthworms, the comedians, make jokes underground,
While I throw my arms up, and we get unbound!

Sprouts in the sunlight, having a ball,
Not caring if I'm short, hefty, or tall.
We hoot and we holler, swaying side to side,
In the soil's embrace, it's a glorious ride!

So next time you pass, give a nod and a cheer,
For the plants in the dirt that spread laughter near.
Together we flourish, through laughter or toil,
Celebrating the charm and the spirit of soil!

www.ingramcontent.com/pod-product-compliance
Lightning Source LLC
Chambersburg PA
CBHW070312120526
44590CB00017B/2637